AF248383

Holding Hands Through IVF

supporting your fertility journey with complementary therapies

KATY HENRY LicAc, BA(Hons), MBAcC

Holding Hands Publishing

CONTENTS

INTRODUCTION

Making a decision to start a family, either as a single woman or as a couple, is a moment of joy that for many goes on to pass through conception, pregnancy and birth with relative ease.

If you're reading this book, my guess is you're one of the increasing numbers of people for whom that journey isn't so easy. With one in six couples in the UK having fertility issues of some sort at the time of writing, it's likely you at least know someone in this position.

So, who am I, what do I do, and how can I help you make sense of your fertility journey? What this book will offer you is a companion for what can be one of the loneliest, most confusing and most heart-wrenching times in a person's life.

I'm Katy Henry, Five Element Acupuncturist and owner of The Bridge Centre for Natural Health based in the East Midlands in the UK. In 2016, we opened our third centre at Nurture Fertility where we offer a range of complementary therapies to support people through their fertility journey. I started my training in Five Element Acupuncture at The College of Traditional Acupuncture in 2000.

Before I even took my first class, I heard a story. You know, the kind of story that makes the hairs on the back of your arms stand up. A woman, pregnant through IVF, had been taken into hospital with heavy bleeding. None of the medicine was working. Nothing. Yet, there was an acupuncturist in the hospital, who treated her and managed to stop the bleeding. The woman went onto have a beautiful, healthy baby boy. I remember thinking at the time, "Wow! What an incredible gift to help someone with..."

I knew instantly that this was how I wanted to help people, without even realising that I was going to be traveling on my own fertility journey too.

Fifteen years later, I have supported hundreds if not thousands of men and women on their own fertility journeys. Each story, unique and individual to them and yet heartbreakingly familiar in the thoughts, feelings and experiences that can arise on the way.

There are countless people's stories that I could have shared with you. In this book, I share the stories of five couples, who have all faced fertility challenges of some description, and the complementary therapists who supported them on their journeys.

As I introduce you to the couples who have been gracious and brave enough to share their stories because of the value they know it can have for you when you may feel alone on this path, we'll be looking at some of the complementary therapies I believe to be most effective in maintaining equilibrium of body, mind and spirit. As an acupuncturist, I'll be covering that one, but there are other key players. I turn to the experts to provide insights into nutritional therapy, hypnotherapy, reflexology and abdominal massage.

It's important to point out, though, that this list is not exhaustive when it comes to the incredible work that helps couples in this situation. Other options that deserve a mention are osteopathy, crystal therapy, body talk, kinesiology, matrix birth reimprinting.

I believe one of the key elements of what can be an emotional and draining fertility journey is finding the right complementary therapy practitioner for you. It may not be the person everyone is raving about. It may not be the most qualified or experienced practitioner. The most effective treatment you can have is with the complementary therapist that helps you feel heard, understood, calmer and more balanced. Please don't think that you have to go and see Joe Bloggs who lives an hour's drive away just because they are the person who's been recommended to you by the consultant at the clinic. These are holistic treatments and the whole experience matters. Absolutely interview your potential complementary therapist. Trust yourself first and foremost.

The reality is, wherever you are on your fertility journey, whether you're just considering starting a family or you're about to embark on your eighth IVF cycle with donor eggs, you know your body far better than anyone else does. You are in charge of your body, mind and the choices you are making throughout this area of your life. You are the expert in you.

I may have a wealth of experience in treating couples in your situation or similar, but it is you who knows how you work, how you feel, and where your limits and expectations lie. At a time when the future may seem out of your hands, you absolutely have the power to take the best care of yourself and your partner to make the best decisions for you.

Wishing you love and happiness, wherever you are on this path.

Katy Henry

THE ROAD TO IVF

Going down the assisted fertility path? Here's a little about what you can expect and in what order. Everyone's journey is different, though this should help you navigate some of the unknown.

The GP

Your GP is your first port of call when you start investigations into why you may not be conceiving. This may be after 18 months of trying; it may be after 6 months. For women over the age of 36, most GPs will refer you to a fertility clinic after 6 months of trying to conceive naturally. It is of course possible that you already know that you have a medical condition that would prevent you from having children naturally, such as cystic fibrosis, and as such choose to go at the earlier opportunity.

Your doctor will start with three basic tests. A sperm analysis for the male and two blood tests for the female. The two blood tests are to determine if you are ovulating (usually taken on Day 21 of your menstrual cycle) and another to see what your egg reserve looks like (how many eggs you may have 'left'). This second test can be done by measuring the AMH (anti-mullerian hormone) and FSH (follicle-stimulating hormone) levels. Historically, they would measure only FSH between Days 1 and 3 of your menstrual cycle, but it is more common now to test the AMH levels, which can be done throughout the cycle.

Once the results of these tests are back and you have another appointment with your GP, it is usual to be referred to a specific fertility clinic for further investigations. The GP may repeat some of the tests, particularly a semen analysis, as sperm can change so much in quality over the course of 90 days. Other tests, such as blood tests for sexually transmitted infections, may also be carried out by your GP.

The fertility clinic

At the initial consultation with the fertility nurse/consultant, they will take a detailed history and perform some health checks. Being a non-smoker and having a BMI under 30 are two of the key indicators that are checked at such a consultation as there are strict criteria in the UK for undergoing an IVF cycle on the NHS. Of course, there's always the story of that woman hooked on cocaine who became pregnant, but we are becoming increasingly informed about the negative effects that smoking and obesity can have on fertility issues.

Early in your fertility journey, you will have a transvaginal scan, or as I like to call it, dildo cam. This is an internal scan of the vagina, which enables the nurse or consultant to use the scanner (not dissimilar to a dildo with a condom put on for each new patient) to get a detailed view of your ovaries and womb. Looking at the ovaries, the nurse or consultant is able to do follicular tracking, whereby they determine where you are in your menstrual cycle and count the number of follicles you have in each ovary. Depending on what they see and what your hormone blood tests reveal, the nurse or consultant can see how well they think you'll respond to medications used in assisted fertility cycles.

Before being referred for fertility treatment, the clinic will usually carry out a hysteroscopy (a procedure carried out under local anaesthetic) to look at your fallopian tubes. Fallopian tubes can sometimes become damaged either after an ectopic pregnancy or if you've previously had chlamydia. Our fallopian tubes are similar in size to a hair on our head; should they become damaged, it's like putting hair crimpers on that hair strand. Once the tube is damaged, it can prevent the sperm and egg meeting in the necessary way to form an embryo.

IVF is the medical procedure that enables the consultant to bypass this stage, allowing the sperm and egg to meet, create an embryo and be reimplanted in the uterus. A similar procedure that may be carried out is a laparoscopy, which is done under a general anaesthetic and involves making an incision into the abdomen to access the area and have a look around for disorders of the reproductive organs.

Possible next steps: stimulation drugs

There are usually three treatments that come next in assisted fertility treatments. Depending on the results of the initial tests, you may or may not do these in order. You may miss certain treatments out completely and proceed straight to IVF.

If a woman is not ovulating, as is often the case for women with polycystic ovary syndrome, for example, you may be prescribed a drug called Clomid for three to six months to increase the chances of ovulation. This is only one example, so don't worry if you're given another stimulation drug. During this time, you'll be asked to continue trying naturally. Within the first month, the clinic will perform follicle tracking again to ensure that you're not overstimulated or that you do not then produce more than two follicles of the required size (usually between 18 and 24 mm) to create an embryo.

Possible next steps: intrauterine insemination (IUI)

If ovulation drugs are unsuccessful on their own, you would then usually be offered IUI (intrauterine insemination), where again you may or may not be given stimulation drugs to increase the number of follicles. You can expect to have internal scans around Days 10 to 12 and be offered a trigger HCG injection so as to time the point of ovulation (usually 36 hours later), when you will go to the clinic for insemination.

On the day of insemination, the male partner is asked to go in a couple of hours earlier than you so as to produce a fresh semen sample. This gets 'washed' in order to remove the majority of the 'debris' (because only about 4% of a sperm sample is considered 'good sperm'). That sample is then inseminated into the female partner's uterus. Progesterone pessaries may also be prescribed to support a pregnancy, should that occur. You're then asked to do a pregnancy test 14 to 16 days later.

Trivia alert!

In effect, what this does is give the sperm a much greater chance of reaching the mature egg at the critical time, taking out some of the legwork! Sperm is able to live for up to five days in the fallopian tube. Yes, we women have an incredible ability to release hormones that send sperm to 'sleep' at the neck of the fallopian tube until such a time that we have a hormone surge and ovulation takes place, sending the mature egg from the ovary to the trumpet- like opening of the fallopian tube.

The egg on the other hand has around a 12-hour window in which to be fertilised by the sperm, so it needs to work hard and fast. The sperm, which has already traveled the equivalent of man walking to the moon, never mind the 50:50 decision as to which fallopian tube to travel up, then has to penetrate one of the hardest surfaces known to mankind. Once one has made it through, the egg will seal up, while creating a magical chemical-releasing display.

Next, the fertilised egg travels down the fallopian tube, with the cells dividing continuously. At around Day 5, the fertilised embryo may implant (hopefully!) into the lining of the womb. If

16

implantation is successful, the progesterone levels will remain high to support the pregnancy. If this doesn't happen, the progesterone levels drop, the lining of the womb sheds and menstruation begins.

With all that has to happen in order for the embryo to be created and get to the point of implantation, life is a pretty incredible feat! It's also not surprising to learn that a couple trying to conceive naturally have only a 15 to 18% of becoming pregnant in each menstrual cycle. During an IUI cycle, this likelihood increases by a few percentage points.

Possible next steps: in vitro fertilisation (IVF)

If you have been unsuccessful with these two treatments, you may then be offered to progress onto IVF (in vitro fertilisation) treatment. There is a possibility of 'bypassing' Clomid and IUI treatment if, for example, either your sperm or follicle counts are considered low.

For some couples, reaching this stage can be where they feel they can place most hope. I have seen couples who have been frustrated at giving up their precious 'fertile time' to IUI and Clomid treatments for such a minimal increase in chances of conception, when it has felt like a 'no-brainer' to proceed with IVF treatment, which can double or triple the likelihood of conception in some cases.

COMPLEMENTARY THERAPIES

Using complementary therapies on your fertility journey is a personal choice. For best results, you need to find a therapy that you find relaxing performed by someone you feel comfortable with.

As I mentioned in the beginning, one of the most valuable considerations to make for your complementary therapy is your practitioner and finding the therapy that works for you, because the purpose is to find support for your journey, not make things harder. You shouldn't have to travel a long way to have a treatment where you're not getting the benefits of relaxation or to see a therapist you don't trust or feel confident in. You need to be able to confide in your therapist and feel that he or she understands you. You don't need to torture yourself. You shouldn't make life more difficult in order to fit this in. As the name suggests, complementary therapies should complement your treatment, not be something you do because you think you have to, or because someone said you should. Finding that right person is part of your journey.

Acupuncture: A Good All-Rounder

Generally, acupuncture works on an energy system with the idea that we have 12 energy pathways or 'meridians' that flow through our body. These pathways relate to and connect with our organs. For optimal health, we want to keep the flow of energy in the system as smooth as possible.

If we keep our energy flowing and in balance, we stay healthy. In our modern lives though, we are constantly asking a lot of our bodies: we work when it's dark; we don't eat particularly healthily; we hold in our emotions and we don't move as often as we should. All of these things have an impact on our energy systems that show up as blockages. I liken the energy pathways to a motorway system, where there will be hotspots that get blocked. These blockages in the body's energy can be linked with emotions.

Acupuncturists apply fine needles to keep the energy flow smooth and in balance, instead of emotions being stored in the body and manifesting as ill-health.

If acupuncture in itself can be helpful, where it relates to fertility is around being balanced hormonally, nutritionally and emotionally when we want to get pregnant. We can become stressed quickly. Our hormone cycles can get out- of-sync. Our bodies react differently depending what we eat. Acupuncture, therefore, can help in any stage of your fertility journey. It also has a cumulative effect, so regular acupuncture will be beneficial in maintaining balance in your body overall.

Acupuncture works on a body-mind-spirit level. It will work physically, emotionally and spiritually. What we are looking to do with acupuncture is strengthen the system, have you in as regular a cycle as possible and alleviate stress.

For fertility, there are many ways in which acupuncture helps. It can increase blood flow to the uterus, maintain our cycle, help stimulate ovaries, lessen or counteract the side effects of IVF drugs. Basically, it's a fantastic all-round therapy.

When to have acupuncture:

Start where you are. And start as soon as possible.

Ideally, for women, I suggest having acupuncture in the lead up to your treatment, at least six weeks prior. For men, have weekly sessions for the three months leading up to treatment, because that's the length of your sperm cycle. Sperm changes every three months and is affected so much by what we eat, drink, and have in our bodies (a virus etc), so eating healthily is important. Acupuncture also releases moxa, which warms and heats the energy and is good for morphology, mobility and motility of the sperm. We've seen massive improvements in men's sperm after acupuncture treatments.

There's no point beating yourself up about not starting earlier, if you are a little way down the line. If you're at the point of transfer and you've only just met an acupuncturist you click with, don't think you've left it too late. Starting as soon as possible will still be helpful.

Hypnotherapy: The Law of the Little Things

When we repeatedly and consistently do the little things, with intent, over time, they build into something great, something real. This applies to negative as well as positive habits.

We might feel that we aren't in control of our lives or that we can't change. If we criticise or limit ourselves repeatedly over a period using our inner voice – "you're so stupid", "you can't do this", "you don't deserve that" – we believe it and it becomes our default limiting position. The reverse is equally true. When we believe that we are worthy, that we can do something, that we are capable, that we can come through, these too become core beliefs and we respond accordingly.

This applies to actions and behaviours as well as thoughts and attitudes. We can walk a little further, we can smile more often, we can make time etc. What we focus on becomes our reality.

Think of it as building a mosaic picture. We might not be able to make large changes in our lives, but we can all repeatedly and consistently add a few new tiles that one by one start to form a bigger picture. Little things, when put together, are much more powerful than the individual parts.

Pre-Conception Nutrition

Nutritional deficiencies prior to conception have been related to certain birth defects, so ensuring optimal nutrition prior to and during pregnancy is vital. The nutritional status of women can prevent future generations from suffering from chronic diseases.

Supplements are not an option in place of a good diet. Diet must come first. This can be supported by supplements for individual needs. The diet should include all food groups: carbohydrate, protein and essential fats, plus plenty of water. Begin your eating plan at least three months prior to starting a family.

Complex carbohydrates:

These supply the main source of energy. They are whole foods and vegetables, which have a low glycaemic index in comparison to simple carbohydrates.

Simple carbohydrates include processed foods like white bread, white pasta, packet cereals, cakes, biscuits, crackers, sweets, chocolate, fizzy drinks and sugar. Limit your intake of simple carbs.

Fruit provides great nutrient values and antioxidants to help protect your cells. However, do not over-eat fruit as it is also high in natural sugars, which can affect hormone balance. Eat two to three portions per day with a little protein, like a small handful of nuts, to slow the sugar release from the fruit.

Eat a 'rainbow' of colours each day. Each colour represents a different phytonutrient to support your body.

Whole grains, fruits, vegetables, nuts and seeds will also supply a good source of fibre. Fibre keeps your bowels moving, and in so doing, helps your body eliminate toxins and waste, including used hormones. For those who need extra help to get their bowels moving, try a tablespoon of flax seeds (linseeds). Soak in water overnight and drink the next morning.

Water:

Ensure you drink plenty for bowel function, hydration of the cells (so they function fully) and toxin elimination. Aim for six to eight glasses (1.5 litres) per day. Increase your intake of water if you drink tea and coffee. Increase your intake also if you've upped your fibre; this will help keep the stools soft and makes them easier to pass.

Protein:

Eat good quality protein at each meal to supply the body with its building blocks. These building blocks are called amino acids and are used for cell structure, immune function, enzymes and hormones. Good quality protein includes wild, free-range or organic meat and fish, and eggs, nuts and seeds, legumes and lentils. Avoid processed meats like bacon and sausages.

Take care not to overeat red meat; it has been associated with oestrogen-dependent conditions like fibroids and endometriosis, and also carries a cancer risk. Keep red meat to a minimum or even avoid it entirely during your fertility journey, if you wish.

Dairy:

Eating dairy products may present some problems too. Milk contains natural growth hormones for the calf's growth. These can cause an imbalance in human hormone levels. You may wish to try alternatives like organic goat's or sheep's milk, which are lower in hormone levels. Natural, live, organic yogurt contains bacteria like lactobacillus acidophilus, which has shown benefits on hormone levels and gut function, so this can be included in your pre- conception diet.

Fats:

Here you want to include essential fatty acids, those fats found in nuts, seeds, oily fish, olive oil and avocado. These assist with cell structure, hormone production, brain, eyes and nervous system development, as well as mediating inflammation. Look for organic, cold-pressed or unrefined oils.

The fats to reduce include saturated fats – those found in animal products. Your body needs some to function, but we tend to eat too many in the Western world.

Remove unhealthy fats like trans fats and hydrogenated fats. These fats have an altered structure, which is damaging to the body. They are typically found in fried foods, cakes, biscuits, pastries, crisps, chips, margarines and fast foods.

To summarise, you should include each of the food groups every day, ensure a wide range of colours, choose fresh, wild, organic foods (the best quality you can afford), drink plenty of water, cook from scratch as much as possible and enjoy!

Reproductive and Fertility Reflexology

This specialised area of reflexology – reproductive reflexology or Reproflexology™ – developed over the last 15 years, but is becoming increasingly popular as more couples' experience difficulties in conceiving. It can also be an invaluable tool in helping to gather information regarding your own natural fertility, your menstrual cycle, peak fertile times and alternative ways to enhance both partners' fertility levels.

Reproflexology™ and fertility reflexology have been developed to look at all aspects of fertility, sub-fertility, conception and pre-conception care. It includes:

- Assessing and regulating the hormone system

- Stress reduction techniques – physical, emotional, mental and energetic (including work-home balance)

- Working with symptoms and causes of hormonal imbalance

- Enhancing the medicated cycle in assisted conception

- Addressing lifestyle/exercise/diet and nutritional supplementation to support optimal health

There are a number of benefits for women and men from fertility reflexology. Looking first at the female partner, reflexology can help in both assisted (Clomid, IVF, IVF with ICSI and frozen) or natural cycles. It has at its heart a prescriptive protocol that works just as effectively with assisted cycles as with natural.

Assisted Cycles:

In an assisted cycle, we work to enhance the medications that you have been prescribed: down regulation, stimulation, egg retrieval and embryo transfer, and in the 'two-week wait' and beyond.

Natural Cycles:

With a natural cycle, we work to assist your natural menstrual cycle: regulation, improving pain, clearing clotting, decreasing spotting before and after full flow, so that your menstrual cycle will start with full flow (no spotting) and finish gradually over a cycle length of four to five days. It can also be useful where there is no cycle at all or annovulatory cycles (no ovulation). It is therefore indicated for dysmenorrhea, amenorrhea, PCOS, endometriosis and fibroids etc.

Improvements can be monitored by your actual bleed pattern, basal body temperature charting (BBT) and hormone blood tests of FSH (follicle- stimulating hormone), LH (luteinising hormone), oestradiol (oestrogen) and progesterone. BBT can give us incredibly useful information in terms of the length of the follicular and luteal phases, indicates progesterone levels and gives indicators as to whether cortisol levels are high. Advice and support can be given by your practitioner as to how to do this successfully.

Looking now at the male partner, the treatment works slightly differently. Men follow a weekly protocol over eight weeks, followed by fortnightly treatment, for a total three-month period, the natural life cycle for sperm. Improvements can be tested by a semen analysis, if required.

Stress:

It is now fully recognised that stress – both from external factors such as hormone disruptors, and from emotional or mental factors – can have massive impacts on our ability to conceive. Reflexology addresses these issues too, because it is exceptionally useful for dealing with stress and anxiety – being emotionally supportive, relaxing and encouraging homeostasis – a self-healing mechanism allowing for the body to reach its own state of balance.

Fertility Massage (Abdominal Sacral Massage)

You might want to try fertility massage, which is a deep massage of the key areas involved in reproductive health and digestion – the sacral and lumbar spine and surrounding area, lower abdomen around your uterus, and the mid and upper abdomen.

Although I've included it here as a therapy, you can also learn a self-massage routine, to incorporate this treatment into your self-care as well.

As a complementary therapy, this form of massage has its roots in traditional cultures around the world from South America to the Middle and Far East. Now it has been pulled together using techniques such as massage, pulsing, rebozo (Mexican scarves), reflexology, energy work, acupressure points, trigger point release, visualisation and 'dry' massage, to make a truly relaxing and calming treatment. The use of castor oil packs and yoni steaming are also recommended (but not essential).

Each massage session is unique and will be tailored to your needs. Fertility massage can be used throughout the menstrual cycle with small adaptations – the womb area is not massaged post-ovulation or during menstruation. The massage can also be used during assisted cycles to assist your protocols, and help you relax and feel emotionally supported.

The vast majority of serotonin and immune system responses are produced in the gut. If our digestive system is balanced and working optimally then we will have an increased sense of wellness and energy.

This massage can also be used when the uterus is positioned differently, either tipped forward or backward, or tilting to the right or left. Although this might not be the main cause of fertility issues, it can lead to pain in the lower abdomen as the uterus and fallopian tubes can become adhered to other structures in the pelvis.

In short, you might want to consider fertility massage for these sorts of known issues:

Scar tissue, endometriosis, fibroids, PCOS and cysts, dysfunctional uterine bleeding (DUB), menstrual imbalance such as no cycle, painful, heavy or irregular periods, PMS, menopause, and digestive issues like IBS, bloating, indigestion, heartburn, constipation or diarrhoea.

Fertility massage is used to:

- Address womb/uterus position

- Release and reduce scar tissue and adhesions from past surgery and endometriosis

- Improve blood flow to the uterus and fallopian tubes

- Improve the immune system as the digestive area is massaged deeply

- Release nerves from around the lumbar, sacral and coccyx which might be impeded

- Improve the digestive flow

- Work on the body's energy addressing any past trauma, blockage or imbalance including past miscarriage, termination or birth trauma

It can also help some specific reproductive conditions, such as:

Endometriosis/adenomyosis:

- Helping to break down scar tissue and adhesions

- Reducing inflammatory response associated with the hormone imbalance

Polycistic Ovary Syndrome:

- Improving hormone feedback loop to help balance and regulate cycle

- Supporting nutrition that helps balance blood sugar levels

- Improving congestion and circulation to the ovaries

Menstrual cycle issues:

- Helping to rebalance the reproductive system

- Realigning the womb, releasing soft tissue and relieving pain

- Improving blood flow

Blocked fallopian tubes (depending on position and reason for blockage):

- Assisting blood flow

- Breaking down scar tissue or adhesions associated with inflammatory

conditions and cysts

- Helping to realign positioning

Emotional trauma and undiagnosed fertility issues:

- Miscarriage, termination, abusive relationships, fear of birth, pregnancy, motherhood

- Helping to release 'undigested emotional trauma'

- Reconnecting you with your womb and creative energies

- Clearing non-serving energies and patterns

- Creating and supporting a vibrant and nurturing womb

SUPPORTING YOUR FERTILITY JOURNEY FURTHER

Aside from complementary therapies I've covered, here are eight key areas where you can support yourself even more on your fertility journey, at home and in your relationship.

1. Take Care of Your Emotional Wellbeing

First of all, I urge you to understand the importance of looking after your emotional health and wellbeing when you are trying to conceive. Having a support network and relaxation techniques can help you feel more in control of your fertility journey, and help you realise it's no one physical thing that will magically make it happen, but the full picture.

We're connected in body, mind and spirit, so when you start on your fertility journey there's an awful lot of physical focus that people will talk about. And yet the bit that you have control over, the bit that you can work on, the bit that you can take best care of for yourself is to your emotional wellbeing.

In any fertility journey, there's a huge amount that goes on in your emotional wellbeing – the self-talk you use with yourself.

As a woman going through a fertility journey, I realise you have scoured the internet already. You know more about your physical body than you ever have. However, emotional support is just as essential, whether that means finding a group or confiding in someone, getting support of complementary therapists, connecting with people who have been through their own fertility journey, or reading about couples who have looked after their emotional wellbeing successfully.

2. Be Kind to Yourself

From a Chinese medicine perspective, as I explained earlier, we have energy pathways, one of which is a conception vessel that runs from your perineum up the front of your body and finishes just under your chin.

The Chinese medicine belief is that the heart is the emperor that sits on the throne; everything works for the good of the heart. When you decide you want a baby, your heart is going, "Want a baby, want a baby, want a baby", and is used to getting exactly what it wants. With every month that goes by, what's happening, of course, is that the heart is saying, "Want a baby", but the uterus is saying, "I'm trying really hard; it's not working". That means there's some disconnect between your heart and uterus.

As part of your self-care, it's important to connect with these areas, because it's easy to disconnect from them quickly. An easy first port of call when you're feeling disconnected is putting one hand just underneath the bottom of your bra and one hand on your lower tummy. Feel that connection. Feel that they are not separate.

Other important self-care practises are: being kind to yourself, making sure that you get enough rest and eating well. Cook healthy food, get enough good sleep and be sure to move regularly. Go out and have fun! Relax and try to enjoy life.

3. Look After Your Relationship

Looking after your relationship is obviously vital in your fertility journey. I always say to couples that fertility is a couples' issue, if you're on the same page wanting the same thing. Your relationship has to stay top priority. That includes your relationship with yourself as well as the relationship you have with your partner.

When couples try for a baby, you can get hung up on ovulation times. What starts as a healthy sex life can quickly turn into baby-making sex. It can reach the point where you are clock-watching and knicker-checking (for cervical mucus) before even having sex. Demanding sex from your partner and turning it into baby-making sex? I don't think there's anything scarier to a man seeing you come towards him saying, "Give me your sperm".

So, take time to nurture your relationship with yourself and with your partner. Know that having regular sex throughout your cycle is important for that relationship too.

We know healthy sperm can last up to five days. We've got incredible bodies. Sperm will find its way up the fallopian tube and stay alive with the help of special chemicals ready for the ovulation moment. Rather than getting hung up on that, use the time to love and nurture and stay connected with yourself and your partner.

You're working towards the same goal. Just take care of each other.

4. Picture Your Family

Both while growing up and when talking to your partner about starting a family, it's likely you had a clear idea of how you imagined your future family to be. That might have been one child. It might have been five. Whatever it was, you will have pictured what your family looked like before you started on the journey of making it happen.

When we're on a fertility path, we can start bargaining with what we want, what our heart desires.

Let's try to clear out all the crap from your mind, because after going through fertility cycles, maybe miscarriages, or wherever you are right now, you might go from wanting a four-children family to "I just want a baby". It's important to stay connected to the picture you have of your dream family and not let go of your dream.

In the future, you may need to work on grieving for the idea of a larger family. Or you may have twins... That was never in your dream plan! Or perhaps you have a boy... when you wanted a girl. But right now, you don't need to do any bargaining. Simply go back to your dream and connect with it.

5. Declutter Stuff, Time and Mind

We lead busy lives. We try to do everything and anything. We want it all instantly. Whether it's keeping busy with friends, going travelling or working extra hard, we are on the go continuously. We fill up our lives. Then when you're in pain because you're not becoming pregnant, you may fill up your life even more to try to deal with the void.

Time to just stop, take a breath and look at how to create space in your life for the baby you want. Here's a few examples.

Home: Take a look at your home. Is there room for a baby? Have you decided what will be the baby's room? Is it cleared out or stuffed to the rafters with boxes of crap and stuff that needs sorting? Declutter that place.

Time: Is there space in your schedule for a baby? Many of us have busy jobs. It's common, in my experience, for women trying to get pregnant to keep going and keep going, pushing themselves harder and harder at work, because if they have their career, maybe it won't hurt as much if they don't become pregnant. Again, taking care of yourself, easing off and making space to love yourself is key. And in turn, this gives you space for loving your baby. Declutter your schedule.

Mind and body: Other ways to clear out what's blocking you involve your mind and body. You can declutter your diet by taking the junk out of it. You can reduce the clutter and busyness of your mind, by avoiding filling up your life with things that don't serve you. You might think they are making you feel better, but I can assure you they're just obstacles getting in the way.

6. Forgive

When trying to get pregnant, there's a possibility of insensitive comments from the people around you. You may feel like you're blaming yourself or others for the situation as it is. To be in the best state of mind for your fertility journey, it's important to forgive yourself and the people who have said anything hurtful, whether they meant it or not.

Here's a simple technique that you can do to put forgiveness into practice:

- Take yourself somewhere quiet with a pen and paper.

- Write down everything hurtful that anyone has ever said to you about having a family, even unknowingly. For example, it could be a few years after you got married that someone said, "So, when are you going to try for a baby?" Anything that has come in, hit you and hurt you in an emotional sense. Anything that feels like someone kicked you in the guts.

- Once you've written down all you can think of, go through them one by one, saying them out loud. For each one you say, add the words, "I'm sorry, I forgive you, I love you and thank you" as you cross them out.

- As you go through them, feel the feeling and forgive the person. It might be someone else, yourself, or society as a whole. Anything goes! Forgive them and repeat the phrase until you've gone through the list.

You might want to repeat this exercise again and again as you remember more comments that make you feel bad. It's the best way to keep yourself balanced and well.

7. Ask the Universe, Then Trust

To call in what you want, you must ask the universe clearly, have faith and trust, then let go of the outcome.

I'm big on affirmations, which means talking positively about what you want to be or have. I reinforce that my body is healthy, my body is doing what it should to create a baby.

I love writing in journals too. Write down how you are feeling about life, your situation, your relationship. Letting those feelings out is important for the flow of energy.

Focusing on what you appreciate in a gratitude journal is another way you can bring journaling into the picture. At the moment, you might be finding it hard to appreciate life because you want a baby and it's not happening. The reality is you have so much that is rich and wonderful in your life right now. If you can show gratitude for that and be thankful for what you have, it allows the universe to know you are appreciative of your life. You will attract more of the same by staying in that positive mindset.

Try it! I promise it's empowering.

8. Keep Sperm Healthy

Sperm is an amazing thing. I could tell you lots of trivial facts about sperm and the journey it goes on for you to become pregnant. It's something like the equivalent of man walking to the moon and then penetrating into the hardest surface known to us. Once one of them is in, the fireworks go off, and nobody else is allowed into the party. It's an incredible sequence of events that happens in our fertility.

Sperm works on a 90-day cycle. It can change so much by what a man eats, what he drinks, how he rests, and whether he is well or ill. A sperm sample you have on one given day may well have changed within the following three months.

Keys to keeping sperm healthy:

- A guy's balls are outside of his body for a reason. Testicles are a cooler temperature than the rest of his body, because sperm needs to be kept a degree or two cooler.

- He needs to ejaculate regularly. Sperm can live three to five days and is at its peak around Day 2 or 3. If he can ejaculate every two to three days, he'll be keeping a healthy flow of sperm coming through. If you're trying for a baby, have some sex! You may as well. You never know!

- Drink plenty of water. There's an awful lot of fluid in semen. Only around 4% is actual sperm. It's important to keep that fluid going so as to keep the movement in the semen.

- Have a good, varied diet with lots of nuts, seeds and protein to ensure a good balance of nutrients is going into the sperm.

- Limit alcohol, nicotine and recreational drugs. I'm not saying never touch another beer, because that could be tortuous. Just go easy.

REAL-LIFE FERTILITY JOURNEYS

So, you've heard the theory on what practices you can use to improve your chances. But what about the people? The real-life journeys that people have been on with complementary therapies to help them on their path to conceiving.

Here, five women who have walked through my clinic doors to get help for their fertility share their stories in their own words. Maybe you recognise some of their challenges, maybe you don't, but in reading these, know that you're not alone.

Sarah

We'd had our perfect wedding, waited until we had all our friends' stag dos, hen nights and weddings out of the way. Now it was time to create our family! "Let's start trying for a family" became our main topic of conversation that year in early 2007.

"I hope it doesn't happen straight away. I want to enjoy the practise." What an ironic statement my husband Adi made when we started trying. After about six months of nothing happening, the waiting game was getting a bit tedious; during this time, friends and family were having babies, trying for babies and getting pregnant without even actively trying. Each month the red devils would turn up and I'd work out again when I'd next be fertile. Yes, spontaneity was, by now, out the window. I was in full process planning mode!

We had the chat about going to the doctors and I phoned for an appointment.

We knew Adi had had two operations as a child, which could potentially affect his sperm. After further discussion with the doctor, she agreed to send us for fertility tests. My blood test levels came back normal for my age (30 at the time), but then we got the devastating news. Adi's sperm count was about 1% of what was classed as 'normal' and our chances of conceiving naturally were pretty much non-existent. We were referred to an IVF consultant at the hospital.

When we met with him, he said there was no point doing IUI or IVF. We needed IVF with ICSI. We braved an IVF clinic open evening and put our names down for the first and only clinic we saw to start our first cycle in January 2008. (Why I became spontaneous and didn't do any research, I'll never know. I guess it was shock.)

We'd dreamt of telling our families and friends we were having a baby, but here we were with the heart-wrenching task of dropping the IVF bombshell. They were shocked too but went into total support mode, with my amazing sister-in-law who's a nurse saying she'd come to our house every day and do all of my injections.

We were told the only thing harder than having a baby is not being able to have one. God, how true that was! On telling my then-boss about our pending treatment, he was unbelievably understanding. We talked for ages about IVF and he ended the conversation with a quote from the Serenity Prayer, "God, grant me the serenity to accept the things I cannot change; courage to change the things I can; and wisdom to know the difference".

Once we received the drugs delivery, we were all set. The drugs protocol was pretty straightforward and my ovaries responded okay; nothing ground- breaking, but okay! Then it was egg collection and sperm sample day. We got seven eggs and the sperm sample was enough for them to do ICSI. Then the wait...

The morning after egg collection, the embryologist called to say all seven eggs had fertilised. Amazing! Then on Day 3, our planned transfer day, I was lying in the bath at 7am waiting for the embryologist to call and confirm my embryo transfer time. The phone rang... Her voice was shaky and it took me by surprise. After confirming my personal details, she said, "Sarah, I'm so sorry. All of your embryos have stopped developing. We don't have any embryos to transfer."

Sick. Yes, I was physically sick from hearing the news. We got into the car, drove to my parents' house and shared our total devastation, spending the rest of the day in shock.

Another shock was to come. We had our review. We had thought the clinic would know what went wrong and were all set to ask when we could try again. But instead, the consultant said, "We're sorry. We don't believe you'll have babies using Adi's sperm. If you want to try again, we'll only treat you with donor sperm."

What??????

We travelled home in silence. No words could express the pain we were in. When we got home, the phone rang. It was a friend calling to tell us their good news; they were expecting a baby!

Now, I'm a true Taurus and well-known for being pretty darn stubborn. I needed to do something to mend our broken dreams. I phoned our GP and got an appointment that day. She was amazing and referred us straight to another IVF clinic for a second opinion. Thank God, our new consultant disagreed with the opinion. He said that what we'd experienced was pretty rare. If we didn't try again with Adi's sperm, how would we know?

We booked in for our second round of IVF and went 100% healthy. I researched vitamins, ate no naughty foods, drank no alcohol. We practically lived as saints!

This time, we managed to get some embryos. They weren't great quality, but we got embryos nonetheless! After our first attempt, my fear of the morning calls from the embryologist was so intense that Adi had to answer the phone each time and relay the message meticulously. Thankfully, the embryologist was in tune with our fear. On answering the phone that morning, the first thing she said was, "Don't worry. It's good news."

The relief! We cried! Adi always ended the call saying, "Please look after our babies". On Day 3, two embryos were transferred. I took holiday from work to rest and not have work stresses. Day 8 came. I did the dreaded knicker-check and there it was: blood.

Each time I checked, there was a little bit more. I waited until test day and it was negative. Devastated.

We agreed we'd gone one step further this time, so while funds permitted we'd keep going, provided we kept going a step further each time. I started to look into fertility a bit more. On the Fertility Friends website, people were talking about the benefits of acupuncture during IVF. When I dug a little deeper, everyone was raving about a lady called Katy Henry at the Bridge Centre for Natural Health. I remember talking to Adi about it and his initial reaction was, "You want me to have needles stuck in me?"

Hello, I've had all the injections during three IVF cycles. Let's not debate needles!

Adi agreed to see Katy and I saw a change in him when he started. He was more relaxed and positive. Being able to talk to someone who has seen so many men and women in our position was comforting and helped both of us. Knowing we were doing all we could with the elements within our control helped with our general wellbeing and mental state.

After three months of pre-IVF acupuncture, we were both feeling physically and mentally prepared to cope with our treatment. The feedback from the embryology team was that my eggs looked better (less grainy) and Adi's sperm was stronger (same count, better motility and morphology) Previously, the embryologist had made a comparison between Adi's sperm and shopping trolleys – they swam sideways!

Round three ended on Day 10 of the two-week wait. Again, I started bleeding, did the test and it was negative. Adi's amazing best friend who has a villa in Portugal gave us the keys so we could get away to gather our thoughts.

Onto round four. Yes, we went again, but not before asking for additional tests for me. The results showed I had issues with my immune system and raised natural killer cells, which were attacking the embryos once they were transferred. I got a new drug protocol, which included intralipid infusions to lower my natural killer cells, steroid tablets and much more. We restarted acupuncture to prepare ourselves for a more intense round of treatment. I was calm and ready to go. I got to test day but then started bleeding. The test was negative.

It was time to take stock of our situation. Four failed IVFs. Could we really   go again? We agreed that our fifth IVF cycle would be our last. Whatever   the outcome, this was it, our final go at achieving our dream. We saw an IVF consultant who specialised in immune system issues and said we wanted to try everything, even if it was in research stages or unproven. Just throw it all at us! I got one almighty protocol with everything that could be done included. By now, it was 2011 and I was 34 years old.

Round five... So many different drugs, it was hard to keep track. We'd also pushed to be allowed to take our embryos to blastocyst. We got seven eggs and they all fertilised, so we were able to do it. Going to blastocyst meant we ran the risk of having no embryos to be transferred on Day 5. The worst part was not knowing until that morning. We got the call that two embryos had made it. I had both transferred, but on Day 12, I started bleeding again.

No please, not again!

I was having progesterone injections and they were so painful that I decided to take a test to confirm I wasn't pregnant just so I could stop the injections. I did the test, left it on the bathroom floor and went into the bedroom for a cry. Our dream was over. When I went back in, I picked up the test to put it in the bin. And that's when I saw it. Two lines!

Oh my God. That can't be right, can it?

I got Adi out of bed and sent him to the supermarket to buy more tests. Five tests later and each one said I was pregnant. Even if it was for one day, I was pregnant! The bleeding continued, but so did the positive tests. (I did a lot!)

I had my immune tests done again and got an urgent call from the consultant saying my immune system was in overdrive and to come in now and pick   up some additional drugs to help prevent the embryos being rejected. The bleeding continued and I was sent to the early pregnancy unit at the hospital for an internal scan. There were two sacs and two foetal poles. Twins? There was also an almighty haematoma in between the sacs, which was causing the bleeding. I continued to bleed. By the time I had a scan at seven weeks, it showed one sac and one foetus with a heartbeat. The haematoma had bled into the other sac and it was gone. Yes, this news was painful, but I was still pregnant with one little fighter.

That little fighter was born by C-section on 3 February 2012. We called him Eddie. He is our little miracle and we still can't believe he's ours!

Initially, we had agreed that we were happy with one baby and wouldn't try for a second. But a combination of seeing how much Eddie loved being with other children and my stubbornness meant I convinced Adi it was a good idea to give it one more try.

Round six ended before it began really. I didn't respond to the drugs at all and we abandoned the treatment prior to egg collection. In my mind, that wasn't a proper go. I wanted my last go to be a full cycle or I would always be left wondering. The consultant told us, if we had one more go, it had to be our last.

In September 2014, we started round seven. My protocol was changed slightly and we got six eggs, all of which fertilised. We went to blastocyst again and two embryos were transferred on Day 5. I got to the test date and had no bleeding. My boobs were a bit veiny and I had a feeling! Within seconds of peeing on the stick, two lines appeared on the test! At our first scan, we saw one little foetus with a lovely strong heartbeat.

Isabella was born by C-section on 24 June 2015. If Eddie made us a family, Isabella made us complete. (Although Eddie still asks if he can have a brother!)

Our dreams would never have been achieved without the support of so many amazing people and we will be forever grateful to: our wonderful parents for helping to fund our treatments and being rocks for us when they were hurting and desperate to be grandparents; our families for always being there, especially my sister-in-law for doing all of my injections; Katy for making us both emotionally and physically strong enough to carry on, for the endless hugs, understanding and positivity; our loving friend Chris for always being there for Adi and for the many holidays in Portugal; and George Ndukwe and the team at Care Nottingham, whose dedication to helping people achieve their dreams is truly inspirational and has changed our lives forever.

Hannah

Why did we undergo fertility treatment? Well, I'd tried naturally for several years, but unsuccessfully. My partner and I were told by the hospital that IVF would be our only way to conceive a child, after several failed attempts of IUI and years of tests. We both had fertility difficulties; I had a very low egg count for my age, my partner, low sperm count and motility. I started my fertility journey at 36. By 38, I was about to begin a round of IVF. I was aware of how your body changes in your mid-thirties, that it would be harder to conceive and the chances of miscarriage were also increasing.

I was late in trying for a baby for a number of reasons. I hadn't found the right partner until later in life. I was self-employed and ran a business. Taking time off to have a baby seemed impossible. I wouldn't get maternity pay and, at the time, was unable to get on the property ladder. I didn't feel financially able or secure enough to have a family. Even though I didn't feel ready, I soon came to realise there was much more to it than I'd originally thought. In reality, there was never going to be the 'perfect time' I was waiting for to have a baby.

I needed to get my body ready, ready to conceive and ready for fertility treatments, so my acupuncturist helped me. She made me realise that I needed to change my lifestyle; with a stressful job and working incredibly long hours, I needed to slow down. My partner and I changed our pace of life and monitored our diet. We cut out alcohol and caffeine, ate seasonal fruit and vegetables, organic meat where possible and maintained a balanced diet. My partner needed to improve the quality of his sperm and so he ate lots of foods high in antioxidants, avoided saunas, steam rooms and tight-fitting clothes. I also tripled my fluid intake by drinking plenty of filtered water. I took advice from Zita West's book and ordered her high-grade vitamins.

As well as my body, I also needed to get my mind ready, address any blocks to getting pregnant and deal with the difficult journey I was on. In my psychotherapy sessions, I worked on a variety of

50

aspects of my current situation, the grief I felt at not getting pregnant and yet the fear I had of getting pregnant. My own upbringing and life experiences made me doubt my abilities to parent.   I feared change in all aspects of my life, my lifestyle, body, relationship and career.

Acupuncture met my needs on a physical, mental, spiritual and educational level. My acupuncturist would tease things out of me that were hidden so deep I had no idea were even in there, like fears and blocks that were hard to admit. She gave me a book to read and would tell me what I could be doing to help myself on a day-to-day basis. And she got me to stop reading things on the internet! And to not get too hung up on every last little thing the books suggested to do.

She stuck needles in me in the right places; sometimes for direct fertility purposes like creating a habitable womb and sometimes for more subtle reasons like reducing my anxiety, staying calm and grounded. She encouraged me to see a hypnotherapist too, so I could deal with some blocks around having a baby. I was sceptical at first. I'd never had hypnotherapy and wanted a baby so badly that I couldn't see how those small fears could be getting in the way.

Hypnotherapy was brilliant, though. I came to terms with my fears of getting pregnant and having a child. Turns out, these fears were huge and very   real though after a couple of hypnotherapy sessions they felt in proportion, manageable and not really present anymore.

I took a holiday before starting the IVF drugs. The side effects of the drugs were difficult and having an operation to remove my eggs was emotional. Going to and from the hospital over a long period of time took its toll. We were aware of the slim chance of getting pregnant but being positive, meditating, having acupuncture, working things through in therapy and doing yoga helped me stay hopeful, which was a crucial part of the process. The change of diet and lifestyle my partner had diligently stuck too had an amazing effect on his sperm. It had quadrupled his count giving us a much better attempt at getting pregnant.

Having a baby meant the world to us. I didn't even know how much it meant until I was told it might not happen. That's when I couldn't stand to be near pregnant women or small children, let alone babies! My partner and I grieved for weeks. We were devastated at not getting pregnant through IVF. All that hard work, all those dreams for nothing or so we thought...

I'm very determined and don't like to lose at anything. I was keen to get back into the swing of things once my body and mind had recovered from the trauma of the failed IVF attempt.

The consultant had mentioned taking DHEA pharmaceutical-grade supplements, which I did. I continued to look after my body and mind in much the same way as I had been doing. My acupuncturist and psychotherapist were invaluable in the process of recovery both physically and emotionally. I had lots and lots of sex and relaxed into a state of 'this will happen when I'm ready'.

The day I found out I was pregnant naturally was the best and most exciting day of my life. I absolutely could not believe it and it didn't really sink in until I had my first scan and heard the heartbeat. My partner and I were so thankful to everyone involved, but mostly my acupuncturist, who had supported us in a way that was just remarkable.

Once pregnant, the journey was a long way from over. My acupuncturist supported me throughout my pregnancy too, keeping me in tip-top condition so that I was providing baby with a 5-star womb. She supported me on my emotional rollercoaster, looked after me spiritually and dealt with those nasty pregnancy headaches, sickness and hormonal fluctuations. Later on in pregnancy when my body began to feel the pressure of carrying such a heavy load, I saw a massage therapist who worked specifically with pregnant women. She eased my aching hips and talked me through what I could do to help myself.

When it came to it, I could think of nothing better than having my acupuncturist as my birthing partner. She had been such an incredible support to my partner and me, it was absolutely what we both wanted. She was called the moment I went into labour, though I didn't go into hospital until several days later. I'd opted for a water birth and acupressure from my acupuncturist. I was so grateful for her support as my labour was long and slow – 57 hours in total! She never left my side for a moment. I felt held by her and so utterly safe.

Towards the end of my labour, things took a turn for the worse as I became extremely tired and not dilating quickly enough. I was suddenly in excruciating pain and baby's heartbeat dropped. I was rushed in for an emergency C-section and was relieved when the doctors took over. As I was wheeled out of the room into theatre, I watched as my partner fell into the arms of my acupuncturist. I was so relieved she was there to support him too.

Moments later my little boy was born, 7lb 2oz, Blake, our miracle baby.

You can read a follow up from Hannah at www.bridgefertilitybalancing.com

Kate

I met Mark in 2006. He suffers from cystic fibrosis and was always open and honest about the difficulties we would face if we wanted children. I knew before we even started trying that we would have to go down the IVF route. There was no way I could get pregnant naturally. I knew nothing at all about IVF at the start. I just thought you had a few injections, they grew it in a dish and you got pregnant. If I'd known then what I know now I would have approached it very differently.

Because we knew about the struggles we would face right from the start, we had to be 100% sure we wanted to start a family. Both of us were. We were so sure, in fact, that we went for our initial fertility consultation and DNA test before we got married, because we knew the process would take time although the initial appointment came through within a week. Our first decision was which fertility clinic to go with, but as we didn't do much research into the options at the start, we just went with what was most convenient.

With the CF, they knew what tests we would need right from the very beginning. They had to test if I was a carrier of CF too. If I had been and since Mark already had it, then this would have made a massive difference to our options because there would be a high chance of our baby having cystic fibrosis too.

The initial tests were blood tests, so quite simple. It was quite a shock when I realised there would be so many invasive procedures, though, like internal scans and the collection and transfer procedures.

Mark needed to have a procedure to aspirate his sperm, where they insert a needle into the testes to withdraw the sperm directly. There was a chance that there would be no live sperm at all, but we didn't really consider this before we started the treatment. Reflecting on the treatment now, I don't believe we would have gone forward with a sperm donor.

On the first IVF cycle, they took the sperm before I began treatment to make sure it was okay. This sperm was then frozen. We had our first cycle on the NHS. There were no embryos to freeze and we only had one embryo to transfer. They managed to get 12 eggs and a few started to develop. We went through a tough couple of weeks without using any complementary therapies during or after our first cycle. It wasn't a positive result and I started bleeding on Day 10 after transfer.

On my second cycle, I began having acupuncture. This was recommended to me by a friend who'd also had acupuncture throughout a successful IVF cycle. In fact, there were five of us within a group of friends who had IVF treatment to conceive. I often have friends now who contact me on Facebook because they're struggling to conceive and they know I've had IVF treatment.

We went through the same cycle again with frozen sperm but a fresh sample of eggs. This time, I changed my diet after seeing a nutritional therapist. I ate organically and took supplements. I cut out caffeine, alcohol and sugar. This definitely made me feel better. I started this new regime nine months before the start of the second cycle. We both decided we had to do everything we could and Mark followed the new diet too. We both felt so much better. Mark's sperm count increased and the cycle worked. I had two embryos to transfer. I couldn't believe it.

Then along came Phoebe.

After the birth of my little girl, we decided to go for another frozen cycle in July 2014, as we still had three frozen embryos. I'd been through all of the drugs and was at the point when I would have been ready to go to theatre, but on the day of transfer, we lost all of the embryos as they didn't survive the thawing process.

July 2015 brought us to our latest IVF cycle.

Knowing how much it had helped us previously, we both committed to changing our diet again. This was because when Mark's sperm had been defrosted it didn't swim very well, and when they checked the morphology it didn't look hopeful, which could be down to a number of reasons. Diet can change sperm massively and we spent nine months eating healthily with organic produce, taking supplements again and cutting out caffeine, alcohol and sugar. Mark did really well and lost about two stone, but we also had to keep him well and off IV antibiotics for the regular chest infections he has related to his CF condition, because we know that antibiotics can have a detrimental effect on sperm.

This was the first time that Mark and I both went in on the same day for procedures. They took fresh sperm from Mark on the same morning that I had my eggs collected. Both of us did well and we had two embryos transferred. I became pregnant again this way.

Changing our diet, relaxation and acupuncture (for me) were a big part of our journey. As for the acupuncture itself, I truly believe it helped us not only achieve both my pregnancies but also keep them safe throughout the duration. I don't believe I'd be in the amazingly fortunate position I am today without it. Acupuncture was an effective form of relaxation for me and helped me to relax for a little time each week. I also had an extremely effective induction, courtesy of acupuncture treatment. I don't think my acupuncturist will ever beat the record of having a patient's waters break before the she's reached the end of the road!

From the beginning, I felt in the hands of someone I could trust and confide in, someone who I could talk to who I felt truly understood what I would have to go through when I did IVF. This was invaluable. It makes a world of difference to have a good practitioner. I wouldn't change my IVF journey for the world because not only have I got the most amazing little girl out of it, but there's another on the way.

You can read a follow up from Kate at www.bridgefertilitybalancing.com

Harpreet

My journey has been long – seven years in all. At school, we were taught we'd get pregnant   if we had sex even once. So, when I decided I wanted to be pregnant and it didn't happen, I couldn't understand what was going on. When I got my period after we started trying, I was genuinely surprised. This isn't what's meant to happen.

When I was first married, I didn't want children for a while. I was 27 when my husband and I started trying for a family. I thought 27 was too young, but at four years older, Dips had been ready to start a family for a year. I wasn't ready, but I was also assuming we'd have sex once and nine months later we'd have a baby.

My cycle had always been regular. Every 28 days, without fail, I would bleed for four or five days and that was that. There was no sign anything might be wrong, nothing to stop me starting a family when I chose, no history of fertility issues. I'd have saved a fortune on contraception if I'd known the truth!

For the first 18 months, I was in denial. I kept thinking, "We'll just keep trying". At that time, we owned an optician franchise and I was aware I'd have to give up a job I enjoyed. As it turned out, my work kept my mind off not getting pregnant. I wasn't particularly stressed, but I felt the pressure every time I got my period, especially seeing my husband throughout the day and worrying how he felt.

I thought I was still young enough and had plenty of time. Dips was more concerned about time getting on, but I'd reassure him, "I have youth on my side. There's no reason I can't get pregnant. It'll happen." After about 12 months of trying, Dips suggested we get tested. I could understand why my husband was keen to move things along, not only because he was older, but because friends who married around the same time as us all had children.

I had a blood test and the consultant at the clinic told me I had a genetic disorder called Robertsonian translocation, which could be the reason we weren't getting pregnant. The fact I had a genetic disorder hit me hard and was upsetting. I'd been tested when I was young, but my dad was in denial about the results as it came from his side of the family. This made me angry, partly because we just don't talk about these things in our culture, which I find frustrating. As a carrier of the disorder, there was a 1:2 chance I'd pass it on, only a 1:4 chance of a successful pregnancy, and a 1:4 chance our baby would be mentally deformed and not survive birth.

It caused me to reflect and I remembered I'd miscarried twice in the time we'd been trying. In November 2009, my period was late and I tested positive, but within 24 hours I was bleeding normally. Then in April 2010, I tested positive at home again and had the symptoms of being pregnant, but the GP didn't find any signs in my bloodstream.

Even with the information on the genetic disorder, we continued trying. Within another 12 months, we had a cycle of IVF with my own eggs and Dips' sperm. I took the medication and the clinic did follicle tracking. I was producing 25 to 30 eggs at a time, which with hindsight was a clear sign I had PCOS to some degree, but everyone seemed happy.

At retrieval, I was told some of the eggs didn't look good and the embryologist came to see me immediately. We'd gone from having "loads of eggs and it all looks fine" to being told the bad news within half an hour: the eggs had no DNA. I couldn't comprehend it. We were told they would call us with news, although the odds of a successful outcome were slim. In the end, from 10 eggs, none made it past Day 3.

We had a review with the consultant who said she hadn't seen eggs without DNA before and was clutching at straws... She asked if I was vegetarian, using certain drugs, exposed to radiation or excessive sunlight. The answer to all of which was no.

A long protocol was set up and I was offered Chinese acupuncture with a practitioner in Sheffield to help ease the stress. I didn't want to do a long protocol, partly because of the £8,000 upfront costs, but started acupuncture and took a few months off to raise money in case we wanted to try IVF again. I was so desperate for the acupuncture to work that I stuck with it for 10 months, even though I hated needles and driving the 150-mile round trip. I took Chinese herbs and medicines, but nothing worked. Still in denial, I resisted the IVF route and focused on the 'miracle' stories where people got pregnant once they stopped and relaxed.

I remember a time when I was crying my eyes out thinking, "This is never going to happen for me. I'm following all the rules, doing everything everyone is telling me – IVF, acupuncture, Chinese medicine – and still nothing is working." For a while, we stopped trying to conceive and our communication became difficult. It took time to get my head around the idea that it was me who had the problem.

Then I found out about the Bridge Centre through a family member, who'd fallen pregnant after seeing a reflexologist. This gave us hope, although I was gutted that someone who'd been trying only two years was pregnant, when we'd been trying over four.

I wanted to do something non-medical to help me conceive. Not having anything specific to work with was a massive issue, because I felt unable to make a difference. I couldn't look for resources or help. With my reflexologist, I had somebody on my side, somebody who understood where I was coming from, who had heard it all before. Not once did she say, "It'll all be okay", or that it would happen for me if I would "just relax".

We had three rounds of IVF on the NHS, none of which got to embryo transfer. By this point, Dips and I had looked at other options such as adoption, surrogacy, egg donation. After the three failed IVF cycles, I asked the consultant about egg donation and decided to go ahead. On the NHS, we would have had to wait around 18 months, and being Asian, it was more complicated, because few Asian eggs are donated. However, we could go private in Spain or Greece, because eggs of Mediterranean origin are closer in skin tone to Asian couples than a Caucasian egg.

We took a holiday before the cycle, which made a massive difference. My faith is important to me and brought me peace throughout the fertility journey. In India, I devoted myself to selfless service ('seva'), deciding that if I helped others until I could do no more, it would be an achievement. I was doing something for my soul, which would carry me through the fifth upcoming cycle. After a week helping others, I felt more positive than I'd ever been. Somehow,

I just knew the next cycle was going to work.

In April 2014, we went to a clinic in Barcelona that had the largest egg bank in the world. At the first examination, the consultant discovered PCOS, which was news to me. I was angry that nobody had picked this up before, but with no classic symptoms, I was a mild case. Knowing this, everything started to fall into place.

We were impressed by the level of detail at the Barcelona clinic around egg donors, looking for the closest match possible, and I clicked with the consultant there, who said the next time he would see me was at embryo transfer. Dip gave a sperm sample, which was frozen until they found a donor, which they estimated would take three to four months.

Once they found someone, they booked us in, took the donor eggs and thawed our sperm sample, then created six to eight embryos. We settled on Day 5 for the blastocyst transfer. Ahead of going to Spain, I had scans in the UK and took medication to thicken my womb lining. By the transfer day, we had four embryos that the clinic was happy to use. After 10 minutes in surgery, I was told I could get dressed and go home. That was it!

We stayed in Spain for 48 hours, then flew home. For two weeks, I cut back at work and was on holiday when I did my pregnancy test. I just knew I was pregnant; I was showing all the symptoms. I did two tests to be sure, but when the stick showed positive, I was in shock and Dip could barely believe it.

At the seven-week scan, it was confirmed... Twins! Amazing! The pregnancy itself was not fun. I was nauseated the first three months, then had to give up work at 24 weeks because of painful back ache, which continued for the rest of the pregnancy.

I decided I wanted a C-section delivery, because the thought of a natural birth scared me and having to do it twice made matters worse. But at week 32, I was told there was no reason not to have a natural delivery. Looking back, I'm annoyed I caved under pressure. I was on edge for weeks because everyone told me to expect an early delivery around week 34. At week 37, we booked in for an induction and had three sweeps in 24 hours. After 36 hours, I was only 1cm dilated and asked for a C-section but the staff kept trying to change my mind. Then when the shift changed, a new consultant came along and asked, "Is Thursday okay for your C-section?" And that was that.

At surgery, I was nervous, but soon heard a cry and saw the surgeon holding up my daughter above the screen. Then came my son who really screamed! There were a few complications with him, so he spent time in intensive care. I'd been in hospital for 11 days by then and was desperate to get home with the twins. That part was the best feeling ever.

We have two embryos left in the Barcelona clinic and may use them in the next five to seven years. We are also exploring adoption. But we are undecided as yet, because the twins are only six months old.

If I could change one thing about my journey, I'd be more informed. You might think you're independent and that you don't need help, but you'll need help emotionally as well as medically. Communication in your relationship is massive. Remember there are two of you going through this. You need to give credit to your partner's emotions as well as your own. But don't take all the pressure on yourself, like I did.

And don't rule out other options! The mantra 'love isn't blood' is what got me through. I had issues getting my head around the fact that my children wouldn't have my DNA, but this will not stop me loving them just as much. When I look back, our struggles make me tearful. It wasn't always full of hope. I have a happy ending, but I remember how bad it got. It's difficult to understand what the journey is like unless you've been on it...

We've spent so long thinking about the next stage, next IVF cycle, next scan, next milestone. It's only now that we can start to believe they are here.

Ali

On 24 January 2014, I needed a miracle.

Not just any miracle... a full fat with whipped cream, marshmallows and sprinkles kind of miracle. You see, my baby's life-support system was giving up around her, and at times, so was I.

I think it was Shakespeare who wrote that he loved a good tragedy and my story is just about as tragic as it gets.

My daughter Brooke arrived in June 2010 and I struggled to adapt to life as a full-time mum. After hitting a brick wall in January 2011, I was diagnosed with post-natal depression. A turbulent three years of suffering with periods of depression and anxiety followed, until finally I was diagnosed with a severe kind of premenstrual syndrome (PMDD).

Reassured that I wasn't mentally ill and that my condition could be managed easily with medication, we started to explore the possibility of having another baby. After seeking specialist medical advice from experts in PMS and PMDD, we were over the moon to find out that it was feasible to conceive on citalopram and that the risks to the baby were minimal. Our hearts filled with joy as we realised our dream to extend our family could become a reality.

We 'caught' within three months and I went cold-turkey on my meds at 5 weeks pregnant. I endured a tough 16 weeks of extreme nausea, exhaustion and anxiety but I did bloom. Our 20-week scan confirmed that she was a girl and that our princess was thriving.

At 21+2, I was taken by ambulance to the Royal Derby with heavy bleeding. This stopped within an hour and I was discharged after 24 hours of observation.

This was the start of our new journey…

A routine follow-up scan on 6 January 2014 had flagged up low fluid around the baby. At that stage, I was blissfully unaware of how serious this could be. We were referred immediately to Mrs Dent, a consultant in foetal medicine, and a scan two days later confirmed this diagnosis, along with placenta previa.

The plan was to rest and drink lots of water.

A heavy bleed a few days later meant another trip to the labour ward for a check-up and another overnight stay for observations. The next day we had another scan with Mrs Dent which revealed that our baby had very low fluid and the prognosis was starting to look poor. I was advised to stay in hospital for a while longer and reassured that our baby girl was safe, happy and unaffected. At least for now. The subsequent week was a living hell. Massive bleeds, huge clots, contractions, watery loss, extreme pain and an overwhelming feeling that I was losing her. This rollercoaster of events took a huge toll on my body. I was weak, showing signs of infection, half a point off needing a blood transfusion. The doctors upgraded my care and gave me IV antibiotics as well as iron tablets and pain relief.

Emotionally, I guess I've been through the complete spectrum. At moments of crisis when I'm being rushed down to the labour ward by four midwives, I can experience a serene calmness and on other occasions I can be so totally inconsolable that I cannot face the day.

As the hours passed, our prognosis became bleaker.

The facts? My waters ruptured at 21 weeks. My baby had less than 5mm of fluid around her which meant she could not develop her lung structure. My placenta was separating and continually bleeding. The bleeding irritated my womb, causing it to contract, which inevitably caused premature labour and was extremely painful. With me and my baby at high risk of infection, plus me becoming anaemic, everything was against us.

Regretfully, I resigned myself to the fact that I wouldn't leave the hospital with my little Lyra Grace. And at times I feel that I am simply sat here waiting for her to die.

To give her the best chance, I faced labour and natural childbirth. No-one knew if she would survive labour but the NICU doctors would be present to assess her and make the difficult decision of whether to offer resuscitation or not.

My darling husband and I faced surreal conversations about her future.

Would she make it past 24 weeks so we could register her as a life? If she died, what would happen to her? Could we take her home and bury her? What should she wear? Where do you get clothes for a micro-premmie?

This situation is cruel. It took me away from my beautiful Brooke, my husband, my life. I had no choice other than to stay and wait patiently until nature took its course – I was a ticking time bomb.

On bad days where my mood is low, it all feels utterly hopeless and as though it's for nothing. All the pain, bleeding, anxiety, stress, tears, exhaustion – it would be for nothing because my Lyra was unlikely to survive. It's torture. Living this life. Missing my daughter. Sleeping alone. Watching the clock countdown to my next big bleed… or the next set of contractions, thinking, "Is this it? Is she on her way this time?"

Lyra Grace Staley was born on Sunday 26th January at 16.37.

She weighed approximately 1.5lbs and was strong enough to share a couple of precious hours with us.

We had her baptised by Rev. Mark Powell and then she passed peacefully in our arms. All her grandparents were here to give her cuddles and kiss her goodbye. Mark gave her a blessing and the staff nurse, Esther, kindly bathed her and dressed her in a pretty pink outfit.

She was comfy, cosy and surrounded by love. My brave girl. My little miracle. She fought so hard to stay with us for as long as she could. She did her best and we are so proud of our angel baby.

You can read a follow up from Ali at www.bridgefertilitybalancing.com

Postscript by Katy

The emotional rollercoaster ride the Staley family were going through was not over yet: after only four weeks of losing Lyra, Ali found herself pregnant again.

The couple were invited to appear on an ITV documentary Superhospital, to which they agreed, so as to have a unique record of their new daughter being born.

In November, little Seren made her first appearance in the world. The family were delighted with way the story of Seren's birth had been told on Superhospital. Seren is Welsh for star. If it wasn't for Lyra, Seren wouldn't be here, so the girls have a special link.

"It's something the girls can treasure when they're older," Ali said. "There's a story of hope behind it all."

Today, Ali says the family is doing well. Things have not been easy: post-natal depression kicked in hard after Seren's birth, but now all four Staleys are enjoying their life together, while reminders around their home and in their lives, help them keep Lyra forever in their hearts.

MOVING ON

Moving on is an interesting time. Only you can know when you're ready to move on in your life, wherever your fertility journey has taken you.

I know women who keep going – have miscarriage after miscarriage, IVF cycle after IVF cycle – who aren't ready to move on. Some don't want to do any assisted fertility. Others will re-mortgage their home, spend thousands and thousands, and search the earth for the right consultants for them.

The important point to remember is to look after your health. You'll know when   it's right for you to say no more. You'll know when you've given it all you've got.

Be kind to yourself with that, with everything. Seek support when it's time to move on, because moving on will mean grieving. And yet, a decision to move on is also a chance to look at alternatives to how you want to live your life.

Moving on is a process. It doesn't have to be terrible. You can move onto wonderful new experiences. The important point from the Chinese medicine angle is to keep that flow of energy moving. We can experience grief, sadness and anger – all of those feelings come into play. But accepting them, allowing them and moving through them is important for keeping yourself well.

IN CLOSING

Thank you so much for taking the time to read this book. As you have seen, everybody's journey is different. And yet, what we go through can be remarkably similar. Whatever your fertility journey looks like, I hope this book has served to make you feel less alone in it all.

From practical information on what to expect at your first GP appointment to the likely IVF options you may be offered, a little insight into the process can go a long way towards staying centred and balanced. That's why I walked you through the medical side in The Road To IVF section. A few facts and figures can go a long way to understanding what lies ahead.

But if it were that simple, we wouldn't experience such rollercoaster emotions, from longing to heartbreak, hope to grief. This is an emotional journey as much as a physical one. It's everything you do around assisted conception that makes it a more or less conscious experience.

So, in the next section, Complementary Therapies, I introduced some complementary therapies that can help you feel emotionally supported and prepare your body for the time to come. Whether you try one, two or all of the suggestions, I hope I have opened your eyes to the way these therapies relate to fertility and how they can help. Far from just being 'relaxing', you have seen how they have a direct relationship with readying your body, mind and spirit for the fertility journey ahead.

Of course, it's not just about turning up for appointments every week or two, because there are ways you can support yourself in this as well. In the section Supporting Your Fertility Journey Further, I handed you the reins on your own health, guiding you towards other ways you can make a real impact on your chances of conceiving... consciously.

It's incredible the little locked-away memories and habits that we don't even know are having a blocking effect. I encourage you to delve into some of   the self-care practices I mentioned that release emotions and let the energy flow. Whether you start by visualising and making space for your family, or processing your feelings through journaling, there are many ways to take your health into your own hands and learn to keep yourself grounded. It can sometimes feel like you go from one consultant to the next, one protocol to the next, one procedure to the next, but I hope you have seen something that inspires you to take care of yourself in new ways as you go on this journey.

I hope also that our real-life stories brought peace of mind and realisations that you are far from going through this alone. These brave families exemplify human resilience through bad times and good. Remember to reach out like they did.

Now I've given you a little insight into the complementary therapies on offer that may help you achieve your dreams, you know that making the right choices and asking for help is essential to your emotional happiness and wellbeing. That's why I've put together some more supportive tools for you.

At Bridge Fertility Balancing, I have a wonderful online programme called the Holding Hands Through IVF Programme, that offers a beautiful package of self-discovery sessions combined with added bonuses such as sound healing and hypnotherapy. With ongoing emotional energy work and a team of complementary therapists to guide, nourish and support you on your journey, we are dedicated to keeping you feeling safe and informed, so that you may make balanced decisions and act from a place of self-love.

To find out more about the Holding Hands Through IVF Programme, please go to:

http://www.bridgefertilitybalancing.com

I'd love to welcome you into our online safe haven and do this highly effective energetic work together, so you can overcome overwhelm and loneliness in your fertility journey.

Always remember that you are the expert in you and you have choices. One of the most important parts of all of this is that you can make peace with any fertility choices you make. At the end of any treatment cycle or even if you reach the point of deciding to stop trying for a baby, may you move on lovingly, without blame or judgement on yourself or others.

We are here to help and support you in any way we can. Wishing you love and happiness,

Katy xxx

ABOUT THE AUTHOR

An accomplished Five Element acupuncturist, emotional energy healer and successful business mentor, Katy Henry personifies her mission to love, heal and inspire in her life and her work.

With an open heart, a zest for life, a deep understanding of the mind- body-spirit connection and a well- honed skill of seeing and healing issues labelled 'impossible', Katy takes the belief that love heals to another level.

She is a specialist in fertility work, owns three Bridge Centres and serves her incredible clientele both in person in the UK and globally online. Combining her intuition and understanding of the flow of energy and its powerful vibration, she enables her clients to be free to live their optimal lives.

Katy can be found changing lives and bringing joy at
www.bridgefertilitybalancing.com